Dedication

This book is dedicated to my friends in the Association of Christian Writers.

Especially to the monthly poetry group called TRELLIS.

You each know who you are and have been such great support and encouragement.

75 Poems that pop with rhythm and rhyme

Brendan Conboy

Published by
Yellow Dog Publishing

All rights reserved.
No part of this book may be reproduced in any form by photocopying or any electronic or mechanical means, including information storage or retrieval systems, without permissions in writing from both the copyright owner and the publisher of the book.

First published August 2022

Copyright © Brendan M Conboy 2020
www.brendanconboy.co.uk

Cover photography & design - Brendan Conboy

Printed in Great Britain
ISBN 978-1-9169000-9-7

Index

#	Title	Page
1	Popcorn Poetry	8
2	Who Am I? What Am I?	10
3	My Story	12
4	Higher	15
5	Imagine	16
6	Nemesis	17
7	Action	18
8	Valley	19
9	Invisible	21
10	Understand	22
11	The Light	24
12	Behind the Door	26
13	Mary and Martha	27
14	First Love	28
15	Tale of Two Carpenters	30
16	New Day	32
17	I'm Not Fat	34
18	This is War	36
19	Broken Wing	37
20	Sleeplessness	38
21	Message	39
22	Love Beyond Measure	40
23	Love Is	41
24	Freedom /Rise Up (reprise)	44

25	Scars	46
26	Fatigue	48
27	Stronger	49
28	The Visit	51
29	The Sluggard	52
30	Changes (Seasons)	54
31	Spirit Break Free	56
32	Delightful Recital	58
33	Integrity	60
34	Grief	62
35	MOJO	63
36	Blessings	64
37	Justice	66
38	Holding On	67
39	Blank Page	68
40	Broken and Outspoken	70
41	Forgiven	72
42	Unaware	74
43	Play for Your Life	76
44	Noah Knowed	78
45	Procrastination	80
46	Red Line	82
47	Vision vs Apathy	84
48	Where are you?	86
49	Parents	88
50	Listen	90
51	God in a Box	92

52	Amendment Needed? (Oxymoron)	95
53	Messenger	98
54	Destination?	100
55	21 Poems to go	102
56	Filthy Rags	104
57	Hospital Food	106
58	Deception	108
59	Storm	110
60	Breathe	111
61	Things Children Say	112
62	Faster	114
63	There Must be More	116
64	Just One	118
65	Tongue	119
66	Spiritual Beings	120
67	Fundamental Four	122
68	Sorry	124
69	Pretenders	126
70	Second Best?	128
71	Let's Just…	130
72	Poverty	132
73	Drifters	136
74	Idiosyncrasy	138
75	Last	140

About the Author

Brendan Conboy aka the Master's MC, was a Christian Rap Artist for 25 years. God called him into youth work and to take a Gospel message into schools.

He recorded 2 albums with Dave Rose aka Kid Kebab under their collective name of Poetic Justice.

God continues to speak to Brendan (mainly in rhyme) as He tells him to 'use the gift that was given to him when he first became a Christian.

Read the full story of how Brendan became and author and a poet in the back of this book.

Thanks

To El Shaddai, Mighty God for giving me a heart to hear His words and the courage to speak them out. Without Him this book would not be.

To Jude Simpson, for her kind endorsement of this book found on the back cover

Popcorn Poetry

Why call this book, Popcorn Poetry?
There really is much similarity
Between poetry and popcorn
Give heat to the corn and it transforms
Poetic words inside your brain,
can also do the same
They hit the spot, your brain goes pop
You're never the same again

I open my mouth, a poem pops out
In the time that it takes to pop corn
Words can make you feel reborn
Turn up the heat and corn will change.
Isn't it remarkable?
Poetic words, thoughts rearrange.
It really is a miracle
God gives me words so lyrical
Do you think that is hysterical?

It's true, my message is for you all
Just like popcorn, you'll want some more
Not all will be your flavour of choice
But hear the message in my voice
Toffee, caramel, salt and sweet
Every word a special treat
God told me what to speak

Chocolate-coated popcorn is my favourite flavour
It really is the one to savour
But popcorn will not change behaviour
Poetic words can transform your mind
The message within now you must find
Open your mind - don't stay blind
Popcorn can't do that, not any kind

Who am I? What am I?

I live with a life limiting illness
but it doesn't define who or what I am
I am a husband, a father
a grand-father, I am a man
I am a son, a lover and a brother
Unique, one of a kind, there is no other

I live with chronic kidney disease
but it doesn't define who or what I am
I am a singer, a drummer, a musician
playing in a band
I am practical, creative and constructive
I hope you understand
I have passion and compassion
I care, I love to share
I am a friend, you can depend
to the very end
I am vulnerable, I feel pain
though I am wonderfully made

I live with polycystic kidney disease
but it doesn't define who or what I am
I am a dreamer, a hoper
a visionary kind of man
So I plan
for a better future and do the things I can
I am a poet, a writer
an author and a scribe

Communicate with words
to make you feel alive
I care about charity, integrity and trust
honesty and respect are also both a must

I live with a kidney transplant
but it doesn't define who or what I do
One day I'll die, I'll never lie
I'll always say what's true
I am a Christian, a child of God, forgiven for my sin
I am a sinner, saved by grace, His spirit lives within
I'm not perfect, I make mistakes
and sometimes do things wrong
But I long, to make a difference
that will last after I've gone

I live with a disability, one that you cannot see
but it does not define who or what makes me, me
I am confident, I am able, look what I can do
not what I cannot
I know my limitations, I'm positive with my lot
my half-full pot
At times I am despondent
to leave this out would be a lie
Though I make the most of what I have
I hope you give it a try?
Not one of us is perfect, no way near
it's way off far.
But don't let that stop you trying or
define the way you are

My Story

Can't remember before, the age of four
Though the broken window, I do recall
Now we call it domestic violence
When I was a kid,
neighbours remained in silence
Shouts and screams disturbed my dreams
Messed up my head, as I lay in bed
By the age of twelve, I sleep with a knife
Learnt to fight - Fight for control
Will I ever crawl from this hole?
Dreading every hour, in need of power
Problem to solve, need to evolve
So, I became a bully, satisfaction fully
Or so it seemed, but it was only in my dreams
Outside all is calm, inside rings alarms
so now I self-harm.
At fourteen years old, my mind breaks
time to decide my own fate.
Time to make an exit plan, I'll end my life,
I know that I can.
I didn't. I talked instead
better to talk than being dead.
At sixteen, I got my dream
Really such a fool, kicked out of school
Thought that it was great, I made my own fate

School was such a waste
only three qualifications
In a life of aggravation and deprivation
Ten years later at twenty-six
married with a wife and kids
Stopped my evil tricks, still something was amiss
All was fixed with Jesus in the mix
He gave me a gift.
Taught me to write, rhyme and rap
A miraculous change and I never looked back
I became a Christian man
and God, He had a plan
Full of his truth
He called me to work with youth
With his integrity, I grew a charity
Followed his vision, man on a mission
Twenty-four years of loving those kids
Plenty of tears, blessings and gifts
At the age of forty-eight, a doctor said
"Your kidneys aren't great."
At fifty-three, a friend told me,
"An author you can never be."
And me, I believed, was I deceived?
One year later at fifty-four
time to leave the project, called The Door
I no longer had the fight, so took flight
I started to write.
At the age of fifty-five, a new skill came alive

Wrote my life story, gave God the glory
all hunky-dory.
At fifty-six, on dialysis
Depression kicks in and starts to win
head in a spin
Two years later, I'm a fifty-eighter
depression even greater.
"God, why have you abandoned me?" I cried
"Use the gift I gave you", he replied
He told me to write, despite
my physical limitations.
"Use your God given imagination
create your own creation."
Writing lifted me from despair
I knew that God really did care
Age fifty-nine
transplant came in the nick-of-time
before I lost my mind.
At sixty-one, now eight books written
I thank God that I'm forgiven.
God said to me, "All that you have done before
prepared you for your latest call."
He called me to write the Psalms in Rhyme
a task so sublime
It blessed me so much, I couldn't believe it
I pray it blesses you, when you read it
Now, what does the future hold?
Only God knows. I just do as I'm told

Higher

God inspired my desire
set me on fire
lifted me higher
Changed from being a denier
made me a trier
I speak truth, I'm not a liar
My God is my supplier
He saved me from the mire
Though I come under fire
My life does not expire
I still respire
He makes me aspire
He knows what I require
Life may be haywire
at times quite dire
I've some regrets
but no sweat
no perspire.
In the past I conspired
but met God the purifier
He made me a flyer
Whatever may transpire
my God lifts me higher

Imagine

God gave us minds to imagine

so go ahead think big.

He gave us hearts to love

to receive and to give

Inside your mouth He placed a tongue

To tell stories to everyone

Let your mind speak to your heart

Then speak it out

just make a start.

If you can't find the things to say

God will show you His way

just pray.

Nemesis

My nemesis comes and chips away
I feel him chipping every day
Every day I feel him gain
My nemesis he has a name
His name is pain
Maybe he's your nemesis too
If he is, you know it's true

That pain, he drains
I never complain
That pain, he gains
Still, I remain.
My brain is the same.
My body is in pain.
I feel restrained
like a prisoner in chains
In this painful domain
I'm thankful I am sane
Then now and again, when pain enters my brain
That is when I write, it's how I've learnt to fight
Despite my fight, I write
I want delight, I don't want pain
Don't want pain to remain
Please Jesus, take it in your name

Action

It's time to take action

Remove the distraction

Preventing your passion

Find your satisfaction

Need to find your traction

It's time to take action

Every action has a reaction

Only takes a fraction

To cause a chain reaction

Make passion your fashion

Remove the distraction

It's time to take action

Valley

As I walk through the valley
of the shadow of death
I don't feel fear, I feel your caress
I excite, that I might
see you this day
Then in spite, of my plight
I delight to pray
And you hear, hold me dear
near to keep me safe
From the grave, I stay brave
feel your love embrace
In my darkest depression
hear my heartfelt confession
In my tearful expression
you leave a lasting Impression
Now, in my deep despair
I feel your presence there
like you care
Despite the pain I face
you wrap me in your grace
Say run the race
set the pace
but my pace is slow
Darkness brings a deathblow

Show, me which way to go
I hear you say hello
Time to follow
yet, I feel so hollow
so I wallow in the mire
No desire
lost my fire
life soon expire
await my funeral pyre
When life is tough
I've had enough
feel like giving up
It's then he kicks my butt
my eyes had been shut
My open eyes
to my surprise
remove the disguise of night
I rise, to the prize, of light
a glorious sight
You lift me, from the valley
Saying, this is not your finale

Invisible

Here I am, I'm over here
Here I am, walking near
Here I am, just passing by
Can you see me? Please try
Here I am, please say hello
Here I am, do you even know?
Here I am, are you aware?
Can you see me? Show me you care
Here I am, the invisible man
Here I am, give me your attention span
Here I am! Do I smell like a garbage can?
Can you see me? Please be my fan
Here I am, all alone
Here I am, get off your phone!
Here I am, in the supermarket aisle
Can you see me? Please just smile
Here I am, I need some help
Here I am, do you know how I've felt?
Here I am, what is life for?
Can you see me? Please don't ignore
Here I am, losing hope
Here I am, a forgotten bloke
Here I am, do you care?
Can you see me? Please hear my prayer

Understand

I know I'm not perfect
I know I make mistakes
Your judgement, do I deserve it?
Do we need to debate?
What good is condemnation?
Just feeds my aggravation
I grieve my own salvation
In your denial, you quote the Bible
In my deprival, fight for survival
As I sink into the miry pit
You talk about love, like a hypocrite

Look at me, take your time
do try to understand
Hear my plea, I'm not fine
I need a helping hand
Please help a struggling man
please don't slam
Will you understand?
I don't know if you can?
You seem to gloat
as your Bible you do quote
Your words punch me in the throat
As I long for hope
Stop your preaching

see I'm reaching
You fail to accept
I feel like a reject
Please don't fear me
simply hear me
Steer near to me
Try to understand
listen if you can.

You don't listen, can't listen
all you do is talk
Tell me to walk God's walk
I can't remember what you say
It feels like you push me away
And you tell me you will pray
But I just drift away
Is that part of God's plan?
Now do you understand?

The Light

Much of my poetry is sad and dark
it reflects some of my life
Perhaps it's time that I told you
more about the Light?
He was there at the beginning
when He said, "Let it be."
He was there at the end
when they nailed Him to a tree
He's the Light that set me free
now He lives inside of me
He's the Light of the World
and that includes you.
Will you invite the Light
and follow what's true?

He lights my lamp, illuminates my sight
God my champ, turns darkness into light
Shadows are no more, I see the path before
(Psalm 18:28)

His Word is a lamp to guide my feet
a light to show the way
(Psalm 119:105)

He's with me walking down the street
and always when I pray.

I could ask darkness to hide me from His sight?
Maybe the light around me, could turn to night?
Yet, even in darkness, He still has sight
Day and night, they're just as bright!
(Psalm 139:11-12)

To Him, darkness is as light
He tells us to shine our light
that others may know of His delight
(Matthew 5:16)

The darkness of life now be confined
Overcome by the light that shines
(John 1:5)

Behind the Door

Behind the door I wait
In prison isolate
My bedroom, like a tomb
Alone in Covid doom
Shut away on Christmas Day
No Santa visit on his sleigh
Please open the door and set me free
From my Covid prison of misery
But you don't, the door stays closed
Christmas comes then goes
I hear the tick-tock of the clock
Then I hear a knock, knock, knock
I stop - I wait - as I – isolate
I hear the knock again and again
Should I open or refrain?
Could have spoken, but instead just open
Jump back into my tomb and stare
Puzzled to see there's no one there
This isolation pain
plays tricks upon my brain
Then I hear the knock again and again
I hear it echoing
deep within
beneath my skin

The knocking on my heart
it gives me quite a start
Then I knew I wasn't alone
the person knocking wants to come home
I open the door to my heart
invite Him in to light the dark
No more live in isolation
Now I live in my salvation

Mary and Martha

Mary and Martha, both busy
Jesus comes by and stops for tea
Martha stays busy, playing the host
While Mary listens and learns the most
Then says Martha, "I don't like to moan
But I'm doing all of the work on my own."
"Martha, Martha, why do you stress?
Mary has chosen and she chose best
She made the choice to hear my voice."
We all have this choice to make
Listen to Jesus or make Martha's mistake

First Love

When I first fell in love, I held you tight
We talked all day late into the night
As soon as I woke, you were there
Gently caressing you touched my hair
You counted each one because you care
My excitement overflowed
like a gushing mountain stream.
The aroma of your presence
even filled my dreams.
Your fragrance lingered throughout every day
Why did I let you slowly slip away?

Subtle seduction, caused disruption
Gentle erosion, gradual destruction
Lingering reduction, divided instruction
When did my love leave my side?
When the streams poured into the great divide
Slowly, slowly, I'm losing hope
Slowly, slipped on the slippery slope

I try to talk, what can I say?
I'm sorry that I let you slip away

This senseless fool, deserves ridicule
A laughable mule, broke all of the rules
My life is so cold, my heart like frost
Can I restore all that is lost?
"What", I ask, "will it cost?"
You reach out, touch me in that special way
And say, "The price is already paid
There's only one thing left to say.
Will you please come back today?"

Tale of Two Carpenters

Two different carpenters, about the same age
Both very pleased with the things that they made
Both men good with their hands
clearly followed every plan
But they were different types of man
Their calloused hands both looked the same
From hammer, saw and working with plane
But destiny would soon make that change
According to each of their names

When they were both 33 years old
Each one did as they were told
One a Roman, the other a Jew
Each one with a task to do
And bring about a story true
The Roman man obeyed his boss
He took a tree and made a cross
Knowing someone would suffer loss
Death and pain among chaos

One would die, the other would live
One would take, the other would give
Now both men had a part to play
I wonder what that Roman would say?
If he could meet that Jew today?
"I'm sorry for that cross I made
With your life is how you paid."
Then the Jew would say, "don't be afraid
Without your cross none would be saved

Without your tree, none would be free
Now there's one more thing for me to do
To say that I forgive you

New Day

The sound of a yawn
the chorus at dawn
Sunlight bright with a new morn
A brand-new day in God's creation
Devastation or reconciliation
A day of bad or making well
You make a choice of heaven or hell
Another day for you to live
to forgive
Wake up
make up
no more break up
No more fight
time to unite
to get it right this time
It's not fine, to be blind, out of line
Do not ignore, what's gone before, time to adore
Love those that hurt you
those that desert you
You don't have forever, to get it together
time is running out.
Don't doubt
do I need to shout?
SORT IT OUT.

A new day
let's not waste it
time to face it.
Time to give, not just take it
instead you choose to fake it.
Just pretend
MAKE IT END
can we now be friends?
Take my hand
understand
forgive me if you can.
Put the past behind
love and grace we must find.
Change your mind
let's be kind
realigned
not disinclined.
Wake up
get it off your chest.
Do what's best
It's time to bless
Forgive and forget the wrongs
Let bygones be bygones
Now make the most of this new day
Take a humble dose I pray

I'm Not Fat

I hear you laugh; you think that I'm fat
It's rather sad, as a matter of fact
You say, look at that bloke, he's so large
What a joke, he's the size of a barge
If you knew, what I've been through
I mean really been through
You certainly wouldn't mock
If you knew, what's really true
You would be in shock
So, let's take stock
of why I look like a bus
I don't fuss
don't eat too much
but the truth MUST, be told
I'm not big because I'm old
Though, I am getting on a bit
Clothes are hard to fit
but **I'm NOT fat**
that's a fact
Yes, I'm over-sized
guess why and win a prize.
If you give in, then I win
even with my double-chin
I'll put you out of your misery
And tell you why, I'm a plus-sized me

My kidneys are gigantic and I mean MEGA
A diet won't help, I'm like it forever
Polycystic Kidney Disease, is the medical name
If you could know what it's like
you'd never laugh again
I know that you don't mean it
when you laugh and grin
As underneath my skin
there's a mass that lies within

But God made me the way that I am
It was all part of His Master plan
I know that I'm big and not a pretty sight
But I still have fight
and the might to write
God spoke to me and said
"I've not finished with you yet."
The pen is mightier than the sword
I'm a ready-writer, that God has called
I'm not really fat, I just look that way
You may, think I'm a prat
but for you I pray
That's a fact and **I'm NOT FAT**

This is War

Tears trickle down my daughter's cheek
A watery sign of relief, then she sleeps
No more siren alarms, no more harm
She's safe within my arms
A new start, new place, new peace
Broken heart, displaced, in grief
Will it ever cease?
We hid in fear, as bombs dropped near
Silent in the sound of torture
Hiding underground from slaughter
I hold onto my daughter

Time to rise up like the Eagle
Run from the advancing evil
Smoke and dust it burnt our eyes
As more bombs fell from the skies
Among the cries, ran for our lives
Out of breath, escape death
Nothing left, now bereft

I think of my man that we left behind
Gentle loving, caring and kind
Is he alive? Show me a sign
Will he survive? He's in my mind
Horror fills my brain
So many slain, such hurt and pain
Please pray for Ukraine

Broken wing

I wrote this after shoulder surgery

I want to sing
Like a bird with a broken wing
The bird's brain says, 'get up and fly.'
She makes some effort, has to try
My brain fills with words to write
So, I attempt to type
One finger, one letter at a time
My arm is broken, but my mind is fine
God told me to write, it is my purpose
In brokenness, He will not desert us
Although my pain is often great
I write the things that He does state
I thank Him for my clean slate and for my fate
I hear you say, 'Give me a break.'

You may be broken, like the bird in the nest
But don't give up, just do your best
I type what I can with one good hand
A message to help you understand
Even with my broken wing
I don't give up, I don't give in

Sleeplessness

Sleep deprivation - Lost sensation
More frustration - No exaggeration
Mental aggravation - Thought deformation
Desperate situation - Try contemplation
Give consideration - Even meditation
Need some restoration
From my desperation
Where's my concentration?
Mind in isolation
Head full of confrontation
Endless exasperation
Sleepless damnation
Complete vexation
Cerebral captivation
A brainless mutation
Weak foundation
Tired narration
No motivation
Pray for salvation
For liberation
For emancipation
Here's a revelation
My observation
My realisation
Only sleep cures sleep deprivation

Message

Another day, another rhyme
They're in my head, most of the time
When I awake and when I sleep
Some are funny, others quite deep
I speak about pain, and going insane
I keep it plain, simple and clear
In a world of disaster and fear
Keep joy and laughter near
I talk about hope and justice
Never any prejudice
Words are my passion
Don't care about fashion
I speak with compassion
A man on a mission
I made my decision
I always speak the truth
Anything else is just aloof
My message is with love
From God in heaven above
Every word is like a seed
Do you believe all that you read?
Don't fill your head with hate and lies
Big or small, no matter the size
Or you will be despised in your cries
Do you really want rejection?

A life of dejection and defection
Me, I chose a new direction
One of love and protection
Now you could make the same choice too
Just choose to follow the Word that's true

Love Beyond Measure

A love deeper than the deepest sea
A sacrifice He made for me
Paid the price to set me free
Speared on a Roman tree
Love Beyond Measure
Perfect treasure
My pleasure
Loving
King
Son
Become
Even more
Let us adore
Love Beyond Measure
We love you forever
You are worthy to be praised
We will praise you all of our days
Now to you our hallelujah raise!

Love Is

(2 Corinthians 13)

If I was the most eloquent of men
With angelic fluency when
Love eludes me then
I am nought but squealing bagpipes

I may quote God's Word right
Unravel His mysterious sight
Make everything plain as light
If my faith makes mountains relocate
It's nothing without love; it isn't great

I could give the poor my entire wealth
Even sacrifice my health
Yet, without love
I am by myself
with nothing else
So, my actions are bilge
without love I have zilch

Love is patient
love is kind
It's not a jealous
boastful mind
Love does not know pride
Love never kicks others aside
Love always stays calm
It keeps no record of harm
Love detests iniquity
But love loves integrity
Truth and honesty
Love never neglects
always protects
Love always trusts
it always must
Love always hopes
It perseveres and copes

Love will never diminish
Though, predictions will one day finish
Angelic tongues will cease
Knowledge and wisdom will be deceased

For our knowledge of God is incomplete
And our godly message does deplete
Then, when the Complete One arrives
Our imperfections shall be cast aside
When I was a child
I talked in that style.
I thought like a child
without reason or guile
When I became a man
I moved on with a brand-new plan
For now, we see a distorted reflection
But soon we shall see in perfection
Then, we will see all things clearly
As God sees us
we know Him dearly
As He knows us sincerely

Now, only faith, hope and love
remain on the scene
But the greatest of these is love supreme

Freedom

In the valley of the lost we stand
Hearts of sadness, is this your plan?
Darkness moves across the land
Pull me from this quicksand
Rescue me, with might
Shine light, give sight
Escapee
Set free
Me

Rise Up

Rise up now, it's time to shout about
Answer your call, now shout it out
Join God's army, blazing fire
Shake the curse of the liar
Follow your desire
Take you higher
Creative
Take aim
Fire

Rise Up Reprise

Rise
Higher
From mire
Be a trier
Follow your desire
You are a qualifier
Trouble? Rise above it all
God is calling, follow the call
No more falling, time to run not crawl

Photo: Geralt Altmann

Scars

Most of us have a scar or a few
I had my first at the age of two
It's true
Accidents, ops and self-infliction
Each with a tale of great conviction
My finger received the first incision
I've been stitched up so many times
But still, I say, "Everything is fine."

To talk of scars may seem gory
Though every scar, tells a story
I am alive give God the glory
Sometimes I make up stories for a laugh
I know it's daft
but we need some fun
My dialysis scar is a shot from a gun
My kidney transplant is a shark bite
Maybe from a Great White?
It's quite a sight, on my right side
I've so many scars you'd be surprised
Though the deepest ones lie deep inside
The mental pain that took its strain
The mental drain I look for gain
The stories of these scars
Are the goriest by far

I tell the truth
I will not lie
I've struggled and tried
Often considered suicide
Glad I am still alive
I survive
and think of those much more deprived

There is always someone with more scars than me
I know of one nailed on a tree
Scars on his head from the crown of thorns
His sacrifice made me reborn
Torture and pain with every lash
The scars that ripped the flesh from His back
The scars on His hands, feet and side
He paid the price, despised and died
He conquered death, then did rise
New life, a gift, for you and me
Despite my scars, He sets me free

Fatigue

Struggling, muddling, fuddling along
Want to feel strong, my mind is wrong
I'm not tired, this is different
Reality seems so distant
I try to push on through the fog
My mind has gone. Where are you, God?
I cannot run, I try to plod
My mistake, can't stay awake, something breaks
Or so it seems, I pass out and dream
I struggle back, breathe in deep, fight the sleep
Over and over repeat, feel in defeat
Energy depletes
My muscles ache, something else breaks
Has my God forsaken me?
Will I see a victory?
This isn't tiredness, it's something worse
Deliver me from this curse
Every day I wake at seven
A struggling wreck until eleven
Four hours in a groggy muddle
Bumbling in the foggy fuddle
Then as the fog does lift
I use my creative gifts
Before my energy does drift
I cry to God, please hear my pleas
I pray for a reprieve
Release me from this dark fatigue

Stronger

What doesn't kill you makes you strong
Whoever said that?
They were wrong?
Take my Polycystic Kidney Disease
It hasn't killed me
but it's worse than a sneeze
My Angina hasn't yet taken my life
Though it certainly gives me plenty of strife
There are people living with life-limiting illness
Would they say that they now feel-less?
Powerless
not strong but weak
So meek
unable to speak as they once did
Lost their strength behind closed eye-lids
Frail and pale
limited but alive
It didn't kill them
they've survived
Hasn't killed me
but made me wise
Physically I am not as strong
But true strength is how we belong
True strength is admitting we are weak
We all need help if you sneak a peak
At what is really going on each week

We all live within our human limitation
We all need help without reservation
The things that happen and bring us change
Cause us to rearrange our lives
New opportunities in disguise
When you can't do what you used to do
Find new strength
do something new
The words that I write have made me strong
A new kind of stronger
a new sense of belong
I have grown with the power of words
God gave me a voice to be heard
In your weakness
look for your opportunity
No more bleakness
turn to your creativity

The Visit

I visited you today, but you remained silent
Your silence has become reliably reliant
You never answer back, yet still, I do chat
I tell you about my day, sometimes even pray
What harm can it do?
It might breakthrough to you
I like to think that you can hear me
Even though you can't respond
I tell you of the things that fear me
I empty my heart of the things I've longed
To say, anyway, sometimes even pray
I tell you that I love you, as you are by my side
You told me that you loved me
on the day that you died
I remember how I cried
I remember the life that we had together
I will remember you beyond forever
I remember all the love you gave
I remember when I visit your grave

The Sluggard

At dawn, I yawn, a being reborn
Slowly emerging, exerting
rising from my slumber
Eventually, lumber
from my bed, I feel half dead
But that's half-alive, right?
Be positive in my plight
I'm not a great sight
But I fight
to wake
for goodness sake
will I be late?
For what?
I stop

and wonder what is my lot?
Why should I rise from my cot?
Do I have a reason?
I've forgotten
Why do I feel so rotten?
The drive I had inside of me
Has driven away with all my glee
No longer can I do, what I used to do
I'm stronger, it's true
I can push through

Though life is askew
I can't lie here and stew.
The day is new
put on your shoe
shake a leg
Get out of bed
shake the fog from my head
Make the most before you're dead
GET OUT OF BED

So, I do the things that I can
I thank God, He has a plan
He says
"Good and faithful servant
I know you want to rest
But you must be observant
and try to do your best
Every day for you I have a task
If you want to know, all you do is ask."
God knows my limitations
what I can and cannot do
Exceed your expectations
with him inside of you

Changes

Festivals, frolics and fun
Sea, surf, sand and sun
Sizzle and frizzle
Plenty of giggles
Vacation elation done

Gossamer web, morning dew
Glistening jewels, sun breaks through
Bountiful harvest
Abundant and blessed
Vibrancy then death

Cold and dark, a time to dream
Life is spent, or so it seems
Misery, depression, all forlorn
Time of death, plague and scorn
Hibernate, in the warm

Symphonic, philharmonic, chorus of the dawn
Orchestral ushering, glorious new morn
Burst forth, conquering celebration
Victorious death transformation
Choose a new direction
New life resurrection

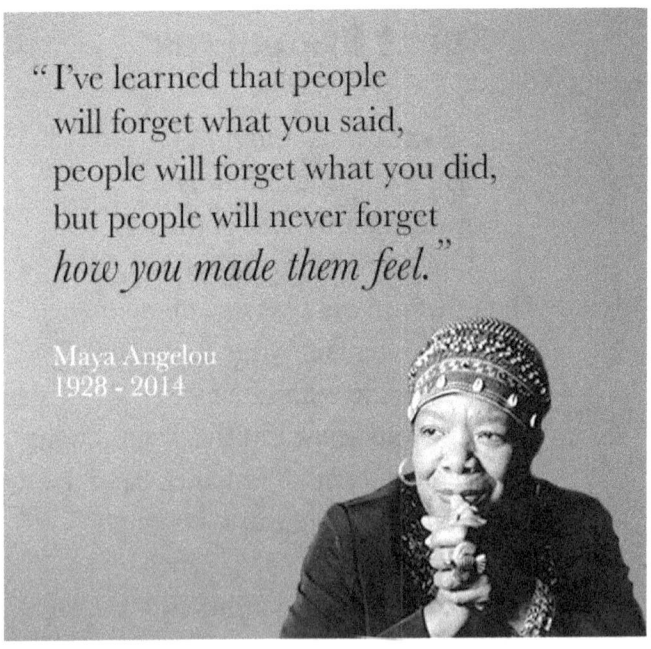

We all have people that inspire us, whether we realise it or not. Maya Angelou is one of my inspirations. She had a mission, with a message that needed to be heard. She spoke out against injustice, oppression and inequality. Her message lives on in her words.

We all have a message that needs to be heard. I pray that my words will inspire you to write and I can only hope that the message contained within my words will become my legacy.

Spirit Break Free

Gentle kind and holy
He is the one and only
Power, majesty one of three
One-third of the Trinity
The power in me that sets me free
I sense the scents of your fragrance
Aromatic magnificence
Scintillating, stimulating, captivating thought
Sensational presence of radiance caught
Sought by some, He can't be bought
Do you want to be taught?
Wisdom, knowledge, discernment and such
Allow Him to show you much
Feel the warmth of His touch
As it tingles on your skin
The tingles grow within
Vibration, sensation, manifestation
Electricity, ecstasy, filled with glee
Tongues on fire
heart's desire
power acquire
Filling, overflowing
Holy Spirit glowing
Quaking, shaking, generating
Touched again I gain, in the Spirit slain

Peacefully I quivered
gently being delivered
Spirit break free over me
Spirit break free
break me free
Free me from captivity
God saved the lost and paid the cost
Then sent His Spirit at Pentecost
At the set hour
He sent His power
The same power that resurrected Lazarus
And Jesus
lives in us
I tell no lies, it's time to rise
In the Holy Spirit be baptized
Then in the name of the King of Kings
You will do even greater things

The above poem I based on my experience of the Holy Spirit. If you are wondering about the fragrance, yes, that is a thing. I've only ever experienced it once and it was amazing. As for having my tongue on fire, well no I haven't experienced physical flames. However, I believe God sets my tongue metaphorically on fire with rhyming poetry.

Delightful Recital

Take some words and make them rhyme
Don't think too hard, you'll do just fine
I do it all of the time
in fact, I just can't stop
I do it such a lot
I write about serious and nonsensical stuff
So, give it a go, it really isn't tough
Just, think about a situation
use your imagination
My garden is full of Dandelions
they give me such a fright
Those lions are so fine and dandy
they're such an awesome sight
They sit to dine
drink buckets of wine
and laugh about this rhyme
No meat do they eat
throughout the week
Jackfruit will have to do
Monday to Friday, repeat, repeat
they're vegan through and through
it's true
What a to-do
it's so absurd, these rhyming words,
at the weekend they eat roast ladybird

Throughout the week the ladybirds do fly
at the weekend they run and hide
How many ladybirds will it take
to fill a lion's tummy?
Oh, for goodness sake
this rhyme is not really funny
Well, if that's what you think
I don't know why I bother
To tell you about my dandelions
that cause me so much bovver
They're my nonsensical, lyrical, non-hysterical
imaginary friends
My head is full of nonsense
that will drive you round the bend
Right now, it's time for you to rhyme
go on give it a try
As for me, it's the weekend
and time for ladybird pie
I spy with my little eye
your question beginning – **WHY?**
I would never lie - just give it a try
It's your turn, three, two, one.
Time for you to have some fun
If you think that I'm a plonker
You're wrong
I am completely BONKERS.

Integrity

Where is your integrity?
Let's talk about the nitty-gritty
Integrity says
you shouldn't do that
But you
you simply justify the act
It's ok, everyone lies
It's comments like that I do despise
Whatever happened to honesty?
Can we have transparency back?
Can we trust all of the crap?
Politicians all call the shots
Such a hypocritical lot
Did you receive the memoranda?
Do you believe the propaganda?
I won't just pick on politicians
There's so much wrong with all religions
So many dodgy historical decisions
Debate, upset, fallout, division
We talk about our sanctification

And live a life of condemnation
Yes, I say WE
that does include me
I'll admit
I'm far from perfect
make mistakes and get things wrong
But without honesty and integrity
there is a certain pong
I don't want to smell like that
the right thing I aim to do
If I should lose integrity
please tell me I smell like pooh.

Grief

We all struggle through the valley of death
There's no escaping being bereft
When we lose a loved one
the one thing we all need
We need to be allowed to grieve
We remember the memories
and times of gladness
They carry us through this bitter sadness
We face the pain
loss and remorse
Try to steer our lives
back onto course
You may be gone and we live with pain
Yet, in our hearts, you will remain
Just give me time and space to wait
To come to terms with my own fate
We struggle on down the road of hope
And in this muddle, we try to cope

MOJO

Do you struggle to find your mojo?
Do you look for your get up and go go?
I wonder, how exactly do I get mine back?
I need my mojo back on track, no more lack
Life used to be so large and full
Without my mojo it's just so small
Will I survive, without my drive?
I need a motive to stay alive
I need a purpose to stimulate, to motivate
Motivation and stimulation to provocate
Find a target, take aim, fire
My purpose, my desire, should be higher
But I've lost my mojo, my get up and go
Will I find it again?
I've searched the corners of my brain
Then on reflection
I ask the question, is this a deception?
What is MOJO? Moments of joy overflowing
That's what I need to get me going
I have a vision, make a decision
Find joy, give joy, that is my mission
With that revelation, it's time to make a start
Despite my situation, there's still joy in my heart
Who put it there? Have I been cured?
I don't despair, it's the joy of the Lord

Blessings

Depleted

Retreated

Am I defeated?

I'm not conceited

but often feel cheated

Like life is almost completed

Don't have regrets

though sometimes I forget

I forget the blessings that came my way

Remember the struggles like yesterday

Each of them left a deep impression

Fuelled my deep

deep depression

I don't remember the words people said

But remember the feeling inside my head

I wish I could remember blessings instead

Like the times I nearly died but survived

So blessed to be alive

to be revived

After my life-changing decision
I became God's requisition
He blessed me with great vision
Called me to be a man on a mission
Regardless of my imperfection
Now, in this time of reflection
My greatest blessing - His protection
and affection
And a final blessing I need to mention
My children and their children
Have blessed me for certain
One day I'll face the final curtain
Then I will answer the final call
And receive the best blessing of all
Until the day that I'm redundant
I pray your blessings will be abundant
May your blessings overflow
And bless the people where you go

Justice

Inspired by
Proverbs 21:15; 24:24-25; 28:5;
Amos 5:24

When justice is complete
The righteous find the joy they seek
Though
the wicked are filled with terror and dread
Be careful of the words you said
Never say to the guilty
"You are innocent, go free"
Then
the people will curse you in frustration
You'll be denounced by all the nations
For those who declare a guilty conviction
They will be blessed without restriction
The wicked fail to grasp what is right
But
God's people understand with delight
Like a never-failing stream
Righteousness covers the redeemed
Like a mighty river, may justice never end
My friend
on justice we depend

Holding On

I'm holding on
How long? How long?
I long for hope, there's so much wrong
Am I wrong to feel this way?
Someone says, "Pray."
Don't you think I've not done that?
I've prayed for my sanity, I want it back
I've prayed for clarity, give me some slack
See my anxiety, it's a fact
I feel like crap
If every problem has a solution
Why is my brain in such confusion?
My heart fills with disillusion
In my broken destitution
I wait for execution or absolution
Then I remember your substitution
Life might look like it's a mess
Yet, you have saved me from death
I take a breath, breathe in deep and weep
I pray, "please don't make my road so steep
Reach out and guide this poor lost sheep."
Then in my dark depressive state
I feel the presence of your Grace
Your light now glimmers in the dark
Is that hope within my heart?

Blank Page

Inspired by Martin Creed's Work No. 88,
A sheet of A4 paper crumpled into a ball, 1995

A plain piece of paper, screwed up in a ball
Someone calls it art, is it really art at all?
A blank page is full of possibility
Picture?
Story?
Poetry?
What do you see?
Does it fill you with anxiety?
Inspire creativity?
You write
you read
refrain
Screw it up and start again
Disappointment and pain
You fold it into an aero plane
Make paper people on a chain
A blank page has no guarantee
Will it become origami?
A roll of toiletry
Or paper machi?
Or is it mache?
How do you say it?
Is it the way that I said it?

Does this poem have some credit?
Are you going to shred it?
I simply would just dread it

Imagine that you are that blank page
The Creator planned and carefully made
Unafraid to express
He made me the best
Even though I look a mess
and am far from perfect
He doesn't give me stress
though I do deserve it
He could rip me up and start again
Screw me into a ball of pain
Blot me out like a stain
Instead, He said
"Be born again."
Are you insane?
How can that be?
Just take a look at John 3:3
Jesus said, we can be born twice
Then He went and paid the price
Invite Him into your life
Then on that day, whatever your age
You shout hooray, with a new blank page

Broken and Outspoken

I'm not tired
I am exhausted
Fatigue deprives of all resources
Nausea is a constant in my daily life
Just one more thing to give me strife
My body is now the size of a barge
My polycystic kidneys are rather large
Like carrying twins that will never be delivered
They make my body go all a quiver
My medication would make you shiver
Morphine keeps my pain at bay
Then I have the odd bad day
My kidney size
it does deprive
me more than you could know
Open your eyes
try to be wise
understand why I am slow
I know that I make it sound real bad
But I'm alive, for that I am glad
I struggle to put on a shoe
but look at what I can do
Look beyond my disability
and see my creativity
Don't look at how I struggle

through the spuddle
and all the trouble
See how I believe and achieve
even though I grieve
for what I once had
I am reduced
but still produce
and I think that that ain't bad
Look at what I can do
not at what I can not
My brain still works, mostly well
I haven't lost the plot
God gave me tools and skills and said
"Don't forget to use them."
Now I do as I am led
I never want to lose them
I know my body is broken
but I write what God has spoken
He places words into my heart
tells me to play my part
He is the Author
I am the scribe
I do as I oughta
while I am alive

Forgiven

There's only one reason under the sun
Why anyone is unforgiven
Just reject Jesus the Son
He spoke the word and creation begun
He made a way for everyone
When He laid the earth's foundation
He knew Adam's predestination
He made a plan for world salvation
He gave His life for every nation
He said
"Father forgive."
He made a way for us to live
He made a path to paradise
For all who have been born twice
Born of flesh and the Spirit too
Accept and He will forgive you
We all live and do things we regret
When He forgives, He chooses to forget
He'll blot out your every sin
Do you want to begin?

Do you want to elate?
Don't leave it too late
Do you want a new clean slate?
A new start that is the best
Your sins forgiven, from east to west
That means to infinity
for eternity
That's how much He's forgiven me
He saved me from a life of waste
Will you reject and run in haste?
Do you accept His love and grace?
Do you want to walk in faith?

Unaware

Inspired by Hebrews 13:2

I see you bake that cake
then take it to your upset mate
I see you with not much to give
yet the homeless person gets your last two quid
I see you in your transgression
yet you listen to a stranger with depression
I see you when you haven't much time
yet you give up your place in the line
I see you and your bad behaviour
yet you're always there to help your neighbour
I see the times that you act like a berk
yet you support your colleagues at work
I see you in times of trouble
yet you help an old lady whose life's a struggle
I see you in all of your trials
yet you comfort the upset small child
I see you and your imperfection
yet to the lonely, you show affection
I see your low resilience
then reach out to those who are different

You may be wondering how can I see?
What you do for the least, you do it for me
Even in your despair

you took time to show you care
Yet you were unaware
it was me that was there
I was in your mate that ate that cake
I was the homeless outcast
that received your cash
I was the stranger full of fear
and you gave me your listening ear
I was anxiously out of time
but you gave up your place in line
You always do me favours
you're a fantastic neighbour
At work, I never have to ask
you support my every task
I'm the old lady who wants to give up
I was lonely and I had had enough
I was different, discarded by society
I was the child with anxiety
I am the person on the street
I am anyone that you meet

Don't live your life without a care
We entertain angels unaware

Play for your life

We played for our lives
It's how we survived
So… So deprived
I closed my eyes
played my cello
Could not watch them go
My Mutti made it so
She told me when I was five
"Music will help you to thrive"
I struggled at first
to rehearse
To learn a single verse
I'd play a tune
hear Mutti humming
I wonder
did she know what was coming?
Across the strings, I draw my bow
I dare not watch them as they go
Deep
Sensational
Emotional
Dour vibration
Weak
Guttural sobs
to the shower destination

Untie their laces, discard their shoes
Disposed suitcases, give up and lose
Stripped naked and bruised
They pulled me from the queue
"Play… If you want to stay alive"
So… I played and I cried
"Music will help you to thrive"
Mutti's words echoed in my head
In my heart
I know she's dead
A painful year in the camp of concentration
Played music until my liberation
Mutti told me, music is my gift
My music saved me in Auschwitz
I am Anita
I survived the holocaust
I played the cello when six million Jews were lost
The power of music is difficult to describe
This I know for certain
music kept me alive

Dedicated to Anita Lasker-Wallfisch

Noah Knowed

Not long after the world began
People turned from God, away they ran
All except one faithful man
So, God told him His plan

[Chorus]
Noah, knowed it in his knower
just what he had to do
Noah, showed he was a goer
a man of God so true
Noah heard God speak
"A big boat you must build."
Noah wasn't weak
so God gave him the skills.

Then God said
"The people make me frown
Their ways just get me down
Time for them to drown
You're the best man that I've found
The animals are well-behaved
So, all of them must be saved
When the time is right
I'll call them all to you
In such an awesome sight

they'll come two by two."

[Chorus]

The people laughed at Noah
they thought he was a joke
But Noah had the last laugh
when they all got soaked
When the rain did begin
the people shouted
"Let us in."
Noah smiled a cheesy grin
"It's time you learnt to swim."
God washed away the people
because they were all bad
It didn't make God happy
it only made Him sad
Then He made a promise
"I'll never do that again
The rainbow is my sign of hope
look for it when it rains."

Procrastination

Let your yes be yes and your no be no
Stop making excuses when you don't want to go
Just make a decision don't hesitate
No more delays don't procrastinate
No ifs, no buts, no maybes
Don't let it drive you crazy
Think about it no more time
Jump up, step out and cross the line
Get ready, get steady, get set and go
Jean Luc Picard says 'Make it so.'
Don't put off until tomorrow
what you can do today
That's what Benjamin Franklin had to say
And you say
"I'm going to stop putting things off
starting from tomorrow."
But when tomorrow comes
It only brings you sorrow
Is that why you delay
what you need to do today?
Is that why you wait until it is too late?
Why you procrastinate?
If you enjoy the time you're wasting
is it wasted time?
Do you ignore the pain you're facing

lost within this rhyme?
There's no excuse, for your excuse
you simply just refuse
Don't be aloof, just tell the truth
excuses are uncouth
The day before yesterday
was when it should be done
The day after tomorrow you could be over-run
I'll do it when I get around to it
but round 'tuits' don't exist
And someday isn't a day in the week
though you might insist
You may delay but time will not
do it today with the time you've got
When all is said and done
more is said than done
So, say the things you're going to do
then do the things and keep it true.
Putting off an easy thing
only makes it harder and less probable
Putting off a hard thing only makes it impossible
Perhaps I should just take my time
and put off finishing this little rhyme
What would you do if you were me?
Stop, sit down and drink some tea?
Just say what you mean and mean what you say
Do it today, don't delay
don't let tomorrow get in the way

Red Line

Written during a 19 day period of testing positive

That red line tells you it's positive
Time to change the way you live
That red line
it spells Covid
I wonder who did give
it to me?
How long before I am set free?
Life cancellation strife isolation
Despite my five times vaccination
I'm clinically extremely vulnerable
Now cynically seemingly a grumbler
I feel so weak and so I sleep
Then when I wake my muscles do ache
My cough is like a lion's roar
Struggle to speak my throat so sore
I feel the virus in my chest
When will I be blessed with rest?
When will I see a negative test?
It's been two weeks of feeling rough

I really have had quite enough
Are you thinking, 'Why all the fuss?'
You wouldn't think that if you were me
If you were labelled CEV
If you had low immunity
If you had some empathy
Patiently I wait for the line to fade
That thin red line is still displayed
Another day I'm so dismayed
If you were me, would you be afraid?

Vision vs Apathy

Inspired by the words of Chuck Swindoll – Vision *is essential for survival. It is spawned by faith, sustained by hope, sparked by imagination, and strengthened by enthusiasm. It is greater than sight, deeper than a dream, and broader than an idea. Vision encompasses vast thoughts outside the realm of the predictable, the safe, and the expected. No wonder we perish without it!*

Some people are visioneers, with great ideas
Their thoughts are so clear
Vision is essential for survival
for new life and revival
Filled with grace
it is spawned by faith
Hope gives vision sustentation
It is sparked by imagination
Enthusiasm strengthens its duration
It is greater than sight
In the darkness it brings light
It's much deeper than a dream
Broader than an idea or scheme
Vision fills the realm of the unpredictable
It is the unexpected becoming believable
Vision is stepping into the unknown
And knowing you are not alone

No one said that vision is safe
That is why it's spawned by faith
All vision must be cherished
As without it, we will perish

Now take your vision
make it your mission
Share it with others and you will see
The world is full of apathy
They say
"A great idea, we all need that."
But they don't act, it's all just chat
Vision needs mission
Mission needs action
Action brings the satisfaction
So don't give up just persevere
If you are a visioneer
Shout it out without fear
Shout it clear
Apathy needs to disappear

Where are you?

I questioned God, "Why is it that you can give me stories and poetry, yet we don't hear you on the bigger, more important issues – like selling our house?"

You give me words for stories
and poems that rhyme
I give you all the glory
and say that all is fine
I know that it is you
that tells me what to write
The sound of your voice
it gives me such delight
You're the true author of my books
the Author of all Life
You give me the rhyming hooks
I am a simple scribe
Your words fill me inside
and make me feel alive

We need your help to decide
Why do you remain silent?
Are you really unreliant?
Where do we find divine guidance?
Is this a kind of spiritual grievance?
A holy silent treatment?

Please show me your agreement

Help us to walk the path you make
Show us the choice we have to take
Keep us from making bad mistakes
If we lack wisdom
you tell us we should ask
Yet we remain clueless
about our given task
Wisdom does elude
us as it hides behind a mask

Now we cry to you
please show us what to do
Then we wait, for our fate
are we just too late?
You tell us
"Don't act hastily, learn to wait patiently.
When you act in your own haste
The things you do are all in waste
I hear you when you grieve
And ask that you believe
I will provide your needs."

So, we make another ask
"Please give us patience for this task."

Parents

My mum and dad did the best they could
Who is really prepared for parenthood?
We should all do better, yes, we should
Why, after nine months are we so surprised?
When your child arrives and opens their eyes?
You can do the classes and read the books
Though nothing prepares you
for the way they look.
They gaze that longing stare
You make a pledge that you will care
Try to share
the burden
Never really certain
Never want to hurt 'em
"I'll do my best", you say
Let the rest of life get in the way
Something leads you astray
You promised with such good intention
If honest you need some intervention
Not just you
we all do
we need someone to give a clue
Some children always smile
some are loving and mild
Others react and get you riled

it's a fact they're simply wild
It takes a whole village to raise a child
It's never too late to be reconciled
My dad
he did plenty wrong
He sure made up for it later on
Show me a parent that never makes mistakes
I'll show you one that isn't great
Parenting is tough
we all do things wrong
We just make things up
as we go along
A good role model is a guiding hand
Someone to listen and understand
When things don't go quite as you planned
Make no mistake
all parents will make mistakes
We learn from them
they make us great
Children
don't exasperate your mum and your dad
They're the only ones that you have
so try to be glad

Listen

Inspired by Matthew 11:28-30 from the Message - "Are you tired? Worn out? Burned out on religion? Come to me. Get away with me and you'll recover your life. I'll show you how to take a real rest. Walk with me and work with me - watch how I do it. Learn the unforced rhythms of grace. I won't lay anything heavy or ill-fitting on you. Keep company with me and you'll learn to live freely and lightly."

You give me a word and I shout it out
You give me a message to write about
Help me to hear the things you are saying
Help me to listen when I am praying
You speak to me in poetry
Most of the time
you speak in rhyme
When my energy has depleted
When I am worn out and defeated
When religion has burnt me out
I still hear you shout

Come to me away from the strife
Get away with me
recover your life
I'll show you a way that is the best

I'll show you how to take a rest
Walk with me every day
Work with me when you pray
Watch and learn my way
Learn the unforced rhythms of grace
Come into my holy place
where I will give you space
My load on you is light
It fills you with delight
Come learn directly from me
live a life that's light and free

So, I listen and I chat
I hear God speak back
I've no set time and no set place
Just follow the unforced rhythms of grace
Whenever, wherever, have a God conversation
Don't force the situation
the source of revelation
When you pray
you make a decision
You decide to listen
Then God gives you His mission

God in a Box

He's there when I want Him
I keep Him in a box
I'm not like other folk
I go to Him for lots
Every week I bring Him out on Sunday
and I'm blessed
Then I put Him in His box
and just forget the rest
When Sunday comes around again,
I know just what to do
Religiously I plonk my bum
upon a rock-hard pew
No matter where I am
on holiday by the sea
I find a local church and I set God free
You can't keep God in a box on Sunday
You lock Him up on Saturday and Monday
And all the days in between
You know what I mean

I also know that it makes sense
To let God out for special events
Every year when Christmas comes around
A special box opens and the fairy lights are found
Not to mention the tinsel

baubles and the tree
I'm sure God is happy
to see such glee
and of course debauchery
Easter is a more solemn time
we take God from the box and think we are fine
Don't want to know about death
suffering and pain
Just want to scoff more chocolate
again and again
Then, every once in a while
we make God smile
With an extra special treat
we open the box and greet
We want Him for our christenings
weddings and when we die
We want Him to hear us whenever we do cry

When trouble comes to find us
and desperation knocks
We want God to help us
and let Him out of the box
But what about what God wants?
Have you ever thought of that?
He wants freedom from your box
and to have a chat
Cast off your box of religion and pretend
God wants a relationship

He wants to be your friend
Don't keep Him in a box
and let Him out on trend
If you got to know my God
you'd know no box can hold Him
Until that day He patiently waits
for you to let Him in
It isn't God that's in a box
the prisoner is you
My God wants to free you
and change your point of view
Do you know what you have to do?

Amendment Needed? (Oxymoron)

Inspired by the American 2nd Amendment - A well-regulated Militia, being necessary to the security of a free State, the right of the people to keep and bear Arms, shall not be infringed.

TRIGGER WARNING

On 15th December 1791
America declared
"Y'all can carry a gun."
This historic law now faces much debate
Does it really create
a free and safe state
The second amendment is an oxymoron
It depends on people not being morons
Is that possible?
Is this law now credible?
Let's strip it down one line at a time
let me now define
'A well-regulated militia' are today the national guard
It's not a bunch of Rednecks
playing banjos and guitars
Without guns, they feel defenceless
Yet, the death toll is relentless
They say, 'Guns don't kill', this is true

Guns don't kill, but people do
Go on, go figure
a person's finger is always on the trigger
Are guns really necessary
to the security of a free state?
Do Americans feel safe walking out late?
Is America really the land of the free?
Your homes are like prisons of captivity
The 2nd amendment is far from perfect
it's a defect
Time to reject
cuz it is a lie
In the last 40 years
more than 1.5 million Americans died
WHY?
Why do people have the right
to keep and bear arms?
When every year 8,000 children are harmed
Or should I have said
'SHOT DEAD.'
Is that acceptable?
NO
it's detestable
You say
'Our rights shall not be infringed.'
I say
'Does the death of a child make you cringe?'
Gun control?

What control?
Too many loopholes.
Look America
look where you are at
Just take a look at the rising stats
Guns make people live like prats
The stats don't lie
you decided
People and guns equal homicide
People and guns equal suicide
American civilians own 390 million guns
Is that enough?
Is this amendment a load of guff?
Does this amendment keep you safe?
Don't you think it is out of date?
An oxymoron is a group of words
that self-contradicts
So I'll ask you this
'Does the 2nd amendment fit?'

Messenger

Words keep coming like a runaway train
Scorching hot like a burning flame
Words don't stop as they fill my brain
They take me high like an aero plane
Take away my pain
give me gain
Words come from God
no I'm not insane
Let me now explain
When I met Jesus
I found my purpose
I know He sees us and wants to free us
He gave me the gift of rhyme
which beats a life of crime
He called me to work with kids
and told me to use that gift
If you don't use it, you could lose it
He told me to make rap music
So, this is the origin of my rhymes
I shook off my sin and followed His signs
Like a steam train coming over the track
The tunes came humming
and I never looked back
God changed me and changed my story
He rearranged, made the exchange

I give Him the glory
Like that runaway train life got fast
But nothing that fast will ever last
Life was such a thrill, living in His will
You know the drill, keep moving never stand still
Until, I got older, over the hill
I got ill
Might as well kill… me
Put me out of my misery
Slow down and listen, then you will see
Use the gift I've given, words will set you free
Speak the words I speak to you
Speak the way I taught you to
Speak my words and speak what's true
I did a lot more praying
listened to what He was saying
He gives me endless metaphors
tells me to be his messenger
I accept it as an honour
I'm down but not a goner
My heart still beats, my lungs have breath
Reject defeat, I've still life yet
New life is what He gave
He gave His life to save
These words could save you from the grave
I follow the steps where He has trod
a simple messenger of God

Destination?

They say that life is a journey
but where will it end?
Please now listen clearly
I tell you as a friend
It doesn't matter
where you've been or what you've done
All destinations are the same living under the sun
No sooner than life begun
it ends in the blink of an eye
Our final destination
is the day that we die
Or is it?
If life is a journey
is death also a journey?
In death, you choose your destination
make sure you choose well
In life, you choose your salvation
so choose heaven don't want hell
It's all up to you to write your final story
You make a choice of jeopardy or glory
Isn't that great?
We get to decide our fate
But don't leave it too late
Your destination is for eternity
so be sure to choose with certainty

Imagine that you are a train on a track
Enjoying life you never look back
Until death hits you with a smack
At that point
the points are thrown
Is your destination known
One track leads to eternal light
where death is conquered by eternal life
The other track leads to eternal night
where darkness brings an infernal fight
To get on the right track you must act now
So, listen up and I'll tell you how
Jesus bought you a ticket
He paid the price
So, suffice, a living sacrifice
You need to be born twice
Make an invite
invite Him into your life
If you want to know how
just ask the person reading this now
If you're reading this yourself
find a Christian friend to help

21 Poems to go

When producing this collection of poems, I was aiming for 75 in total. When I thought that I had 21 poems to go, it reminded me of a song from the 90's called 21 Seconds to go. Then I thought about how long we have to wait before the return of the King. This also contains elements of the five parables about the second coming.

How long until the show?
If only we could know?
Is it just 21 poems to go?
The day and hour is unknown
Get ready
stay ready
get off your phone
Will he come like a cyclone?
No
Like a thief in the night
Yes
It's hard never ever knowing
What if He came after
the next 21 poems?
Are you ready?
Are you reborn?
These poems pop out like popping corn
Can you imagine
a thief is bragging

Saying
"I'll be round at ten."
Would you get ready then?
Would you stand at the door and wait?
Just a 21-poem wait
What if you were the housemaid?
Would you run away afraid
and dismayed?
If you are a member of the Church
Be sure not to be left in the lurch
Do all the things that you have to do
Or He will say
"I never knew you."
God gives you your talent and skill
Use them to get ready
you know the drill
If there was just 21 poems to go
Would you get ready and let others know?
But there is no knowing
That is the thing
Just be ready to meet the King

Filthy Rags

Inspired by Isaiah 64:6

Have you ever thought that you know best?
That your way is better than all the rest?
You may be strong with great capabilities
Yet
We are also weak with disabilities
A blind man once said to me
"Not one of us is perfect."
Though he was blind, he could see
that none are really worth it
Here's an example of how many of us crumble
We don't like to ask for help
don't like to be too humble
So
We struggle on and do things wrong
We make a stinky pong
and hide behind a song
You sing out
"I'm on a mission, I'm God sent."
Then
you do all things in your own strength
Instead of asking God to help
We push Him aside and do it ourselves
As if we have something to gain
We struggle on through the pain

Can this be sustained?
Then
on the edge of burning out
In creeps doubt
and you shout
"God, why have you deserted me?"
"You think you can do it perfectly."
Comes the reply and I sigh

Our righteous acts are like filthy rags
With God's help
we can relax
And that is a fact
When this happened to me
I discovered what would set me free
I read Nehemiah 8 verse 10
Things haven't been the same again
Do you want to know what it said?
'The joy of the Lord is my strength', I read
So
instead of strength
I asked for joy and started to rejoice
The rags soon went now I enjoy
listening to God's voice

Hospital Food

Inspired by Psalm 34:8
Oh taste and see that the Lord is good: blessed is the
man that trusts in Him.

I've stayed in hospital many times
and the food was pretty good
Yet
some patients are ungrateful
and say it tastes like wood
I say
"It's still a beautiful day in the neighbourhood."
Some people look at the ice cream
and still they have a moan
I roll over on my bed
and try my best not to groan
Some think it's like a hotel
order tea and biscuits all the time
The nurses always smile and say
"That really is just fine."
My favourite food in hospital
hast to be the yoghurt
They buy it in from Scotland
from a company called McRobert
I can't get enough of the stuff
it's just so lush
As for all the other food

I say
"Taste and see that it is good."

One day, when my food didn't arrive
They offered me a choice of what was supplied
Other food had been sent
This is how the conversation went
"Do you like rhubarb crumble?"
"No, it makes my tummy grumble."
I hadn't ate rhubarb since I was a kid
The nurse just smiled and removed the lid
"This is the very last pud.
Taste and see that it is good."
I was starving so I had to eat
Opened my mouth
closed my eyes
Wow what a treat
With a dollop of custard on the side
it tasted oh so sweet
I've never found a better
rhubarb crumble to replace it
Hospital food is good
but I hope you never get to taste it

Deception

The phone rang
a foreign man
"I'm from Ebay", I am
I sensed a scam
I let him have his say
"Your order will arrive today."
I tell him, with a grin
"I've not ordered anything."
"It was ordered from Reading."
I knew that it was a deception
Still gave the man a nice reception
"Thank you for that information."
Then
he read his script exact
I could smell that stinking rat
As he continued with his chat
They often hang up with what I did next
This man continued and tried his best
He would hear the truth before he left
"Why are you lying?"
I simply asked
The man kept talking
stayed on task
"Why are you lying?"
I asked again

It caused him to refrain
"No, I'm not. Why do you think that?"
"I know and God knows and that's a fact.
Despite not speaking true, He will forgive you."
"How do you know?"
he said
He meant, how did I know he was lying
At this point I was almost crying
I had said, "He will forgive you."
He had said
"How do you know?"
"God gave us His Son, that's how I know
He forgives through Jesus, that is so
You can repent for all your sin.
Just ask now, let Jesus in."
Then he said
"Yes, I know all of that.
I'm from Ebay."
Then continued with his chat
I'd given him the Gospel word
But had he really heard?
It felt rather absurd
I knew about his false intention
But he didn't hang up when God was mentioned
Was this a Holy intervention?
In the end, I asked him what I should do
He said, "I'm just telling you."
Ah well, at least he heard what's true

Storm

How God spoke to me today

You've been a faithful soldier
The storm will soon be over
You've struggled to get older
Feeling so much colder
Like a warrior on a battlefield
You persevered and did not yield
On water you've been walking
Listening to me talking
You have been rewarding
I've watched you as you've tried
I've heard you when you cried
I've been right by your side
The storm will soon subside
I've heard you when you pray
A new season is on the way
Nothing will stay the same
Are you ready for a change?
After the storm, the sun will shine
Are you ready? Watch the signs
Get ready for a breakthrough
I will not forsake you
In the storms, you find a rainbow
My promise is
I'll never let go

Breathe

We all need oxygen to breathe
I hope you're all agreed…
on that
I hope you agree with the rest of this chat
The word of The Lord we need to read
So
why do you struggle with this deed
Do you take it or leave it, is that the reason why
If you don't breathe oxygen, you will die
It's the same with the Bible, it must be read
Breathe in the word or you're spiritually dead
That's right, you heard what I said
The word of God is like oxygen
Hold your breath until I say when
How long would you last?
If I didn't say when, you would gasp
We can hold our breath for minutes – a couple
Try much longer and you're in trouble
So, we breathe all of the time - naturally
But the Bible is discarded absently
It doesn't enter your mind
Don't read it any time
Here comes spiritual death
Breathe or be bereft

Things Children Say

*Inspired by actual things
children have said and written*

In the book of Guinness
God made the world and was tired
So
He decided to take the Sabbath off and retired
Adam and Eve were created from an apple tree
This was the start of history
Noah built the ark and his wife was Joan
Joan of Ark loved her home
They invited the animals on in pear trees
I know this rhyme is a little bit crazy
But it's what children say
Lot's wife was a pillar of salt during the day
But a ball of fire at night
None of this is right
The Jews, throughout history in general
Have had trouble with unsympathetic genitals
Moses set the Jews free
through the Red Sea
The Egyptians were all drowned in dessert
None of the Jews were hurt
Afterwards
they made unleavened bread in obedience
This is bread made without ingredients

Moses did decide
to climb mount cyanide
That's where ten commandments were given
The first was when Eve told Adam
to eat the fruit forbidden
The seventh is
'thou shalt not admit adultery.'
Please don't take this rhyme seriously
David was a Hebrew king with desires
He was skilled at playing the liar
He fought the Finkelsteins
A race of people in biblical times
Solomon had 300 wives and 700 porcupines
When Mary found out she was Jesus's mum
The Magna Carta was sung
Three wise guys
from the east side
arrived
They found Jesus and the manager inside
Jesus was born because
Mary had an immaculate contraption
I hope this nonsense has been a little distraction

Faster

Faster and faster
the world turns faster
There you have it, that's a lie
If the world turned faster, we all would die
If it turned slower
it would be the same
Do I really need to explain?
The speed we need it was decreed
by the Master Creator
The world rotates at a set rate
not slower or greater
What exactly do we mean by
the world turns faster?
Are we out of control
and heading for disaster?
We live in a world of instant fix
and silicon chips
We say that it makes sense
to use artificial intelligence
We use robot mowers to cut the grass
and we like self-cleaning glass
We use mixers and blenders
fixers and senders
Emails have reduced communication time
Then we spend that time online

We search for the latest gadget
We say we really MUST have it
Isn't it tragic?
Our voice commands
and we hear music
Our choice expands
and we abuse it
We eat microwave meals PING ready in five
It's all we need to stay alive
We just like to live faster
drive faster
eat faster
Then with so much time to spare
we get plastered
Drunk as a skunk-like punk
and do a bunk
Life just got too fast
it wasn't gonna last
Any disaster forecaster will explain
it isn't a game
Going faster like a rocket blaster
can't be sustained
Rockets burn and so will you
along with your gadgets too
In search of an answer
you ask the Master
what is it I should do?

There Must be More

Work, eat, sleep, repeat
Work, eat, sleep, repeat
There must be more than this routine?
Are we more than cogs in a machine?
Are we dependent on caffeine?
Scrub, pub, grub and dream
There must be more than this routine
Work, eat, sleep, repeat
Incomplete you feel downbeat
You retreat, indiscreet, want a treat
Feel like roaring, life is boring
should be off exploring
Want to discover, recover, find another life
Escape the strife, be suffice, to be concise
I want a life that's nice
but at what price?
Work, eat, sleep, repeat
I can't take much more of this
I need bliss, someone to kiss
do you get the gist?
Need liberation, new sensation
I need salvation
From the grind, lost my mind
Break these confines
I bare no grudge, need to budge

Escape the sludge and drudgery
Escape to fantasy
Is this my lot, my slot, what I've got?
I want a yacht, I've lost the plot
Work, eat, sleep, repeat
Work, eat, sleep, DEFEAT
There must be more to life than this?
From this boring life exist
Fill my place of empty
replace it with plenty?
Please change my repetition
my hollow condition
To a new position with greater vision
Please God make me your mission
Is there more to life than this?

Just One
Inspired by James 2

If I helped just one person every day?
It doesn't have to be in a massive way
It could be little things like holding a door
Or helping someone whose health is poor
Giving a lift in your car, not far
They say, "Thank you, you're a star."
Just think where you could begin
Take out a neighbour's bin and get it in
Don't make it a big deal, just keep it real
Share your knowledge with others in need
Show them how, watch where it leads
Give helpful advice, be nice
It doesn't have to be a sacrifice
You could give someone an old book
Better still teach them to cook
Then they will feed themselves
And go and teach someone else
Or bake a mate a cake
Don't let the day go to waste
Have a go, step out in faith
Work in faith 24/7
But good deeds don't get you into heaven
Salvation faith brings deeds of grace
Faith without works is a dead faith

Tongue

Inspired by James 3:3-10

It's small but powerfully strong
Has the power of right or wrong
In the mouth of a liar
It sets the world on fire
Just a small remark
Is like a deadly spark

Take a horses bit it does direct
It's small with great effect
Man and horse connect
Take a mighty ship with sails
It's driven as the wind prevails
Yet a small rudder steers the ship
At the captain's fingertip
He tells it where to go
The rudder makes it so

All animals have been tamed by man
Yet, the tongue is a beast that no one can
The tongue is full of venom and worse
It praises God, but men are cursed
It is evil unrehearsed - It puts itself first
The same mouth will cuss and praise
This is not the way
Be careful what you say

Spiritual beings

Some people live a fantasy dream
Not everyone is who they seem
Not everyone is squeaky clean
We show but we do not tell
We kid ourselves and say we're well
We're Spiritual beings – living in a human shell

Never express how we feel
Stiff upper lip like a man of steel
You face an ordeal
never reveal
you know the deal
Why can't you just be real?
We're unhappy that we look so spotty
We get older and feel so soggy
We distract our minds with a hobby
We're Spiritual beings – living in a human body

You get old and feel like an antique
Disguise your look in a chic boutique
Feel weak
scared to speak
feel like a freak
You are your worse critique
yet you are unique

**We're Spiritual beings –
living in a human physique**

Nothing in life ever makes sense
We live a life of fake pretence
We keep everyone at a distance
Why do we show such resistance?
**We're Spiritual beings –
living in a human existence**

We live like icebergs
with unseen ice
We feel like nothing is suffice
We condemn and self-sacrifice
Living on the edge of a knife
We all live with strife
**We're Spiritual beings –
living in a human life**

You may not be agreeing
We're in the world sightseeing
**We're all spiritual beings
And we all need freeing**

Fundamental Four

We all have four fundamental needs
If one of them is missing you mentally bleed
Our minds, bodies and spirits
require a balanced state
When the balance is out
we discombobulate
It doesn't feel great and wonder why?
These four things help us to get by
Not one should be denied

I'll explain these four to you so fervently
We all need to live in harmony
we all need certainty
Certainty is the number one need
We need certainty so take heed
We need things that we expect
We rely upon things being correct
We need the status quo
things that you know

In direct contrast to certainty
we also need uncertainty
Switch up the mix with some variety
Pitch up your fix with diversity
We need to expect the unexpected

It prevents us from being disaffected
Not everything should be predictable
Take a break from traditional
Is it unthinkable?

Next comes connect
to connect to each other
We all need another
to help us discover
Who we are
Not judge us as bizarre
We don't need rejection
We need affection and connection
It gives us direction and protection
On reflection
connection gives you good reception

When you connect you feel significant
This fourth need makes you feel magnificent
Significance increases self-esteem
Your value rises like a dream to extreme
You know you make a difference
Because of your significance
No longer live in ignorance

Sorry

Why is sorry a hard word to say
You don't mean it but say it anyway
You say sorry and pray
Pray to a God you don't believe in
You say sorry with a grin
You pray but you don't mean it
Sorry needs action and we've not seen it
Sorry is much more than a simple word
That you think needs to be heard
Sorry means that you put things right
Sorry means that you end the fight
Sorry without action is simply trite
When you say sorry
Be genuine
Stop the bickering
Stop remembering
Stop pretending
and assembling your lies
You might be a little surprised
Your sorry without action is so transparent

Do you care that you're so arrogant?
Don't just say sorry
you must show it
Then we might begin to know it
We don't want false gestures grand
Don't say sorry on command
Do you understand?
Will you say sorry and shake hands?
When you're really sorry it is in your heart
Are we ready for a new start?
Sorry is changing how you live
Sorry is ready to forgive

Pretenders

Image is all about protection from detection
It's a projection to hide the fear of rejection
It's a natural defence
it's a pretence
Why do so many people pretend?
Afraid to be real and amend

Why do people eat
plant-based pretend meat?
Sausage, burger, bacon, even chicken
Are they flipping tripping?
Need to get a gripping
I get it, don't get me wrong
Pretend meat helps people belong

And now we have pretend cyclists
They ride electric byclists
that's a pretend word
Yikes! They give me such a fright
Those lazy, crazy
speeding bikes
They're supercharged past the limit
I know
BONKERS innit?

Let's talk about serious contenders for pretenders
So-called friends
they drive you round the bend
Are they befrienders or offenders?
Do they cause you to surrender?
Real friends don't do that
they want to sit and chat
Never want anything back
A good friend doesn't pretend

This last pretend condition
is the worst imagined position
Some people pretend to be a Christian
They think it's all about religion
Though in my defending
they aren't really pretending
Be good
do church
be kind
The blind lead the blind
They pretend until they know the TRUTH
Then they are known by their fruit

Second Best?

A good marriage needs time to invest
Being single isn't second best
Regard being single as being blessed
For some
marriage is a life of stress
Work hard to impress and rarely rest
When you are single
you are free to mingle
Is being single really that bad?
Does it make you really sad?
Are you single lonely and grieved?
Get married if that is what you need
Adam was lonely, so God made Eve
Marriage is great if you can find
Someone who is loving
gentle and kind
Don't be blind.
Don't put up with
don't make do
Miss or mister right is right for you
How do you know if they are right?
How often do you fight?
Is there trust and respect?
If no
you must just reject

Being single isn't second best
Being married is a life-long test
Not all tests are a guaranteed pass
You work hard to make it last
Don't debate
if it's too late
Let destiny, kismet or fate
Show you your soul mate
Does God want you to wait?
Fifty percent of marriages are a disaster
Make sure you choose a loving-laster
Don't be tempted
by who comes along
You'll be tormented
when you choose wrong
It's not a contest
don't guess
make a mess
Don't get depressed
or obsessed
Being single really isn't second best

Let's Just...

Let's **just**

stop using the word **just** as a throw-away

We use it in such a way

it belittles what we say

Especially when we pray

we say

"Let's **just** pray"

I'm **just** saying

there's no such thing as **just** praying

We should pray **just**ly

and that we must be

Do you pray for the blind to **just** see?

Praying is much bigger than **just** something

Prayer is communicating

It's petitioning

it's asking

it's reflecting

it's giving in

We say

"God, can you **just** do this?
God, can you **just** do that?"
We say it all matter of fact
When we pray
it's a real big deal
How do you think God must feel?
Please God, **just** heal
Please God, **just** provide
Are you being denied?
Please God, **just** give me work
Just nothing that gets me covered in dirt
Just give me an easy position
Just stop praying with conditions
Instead of saying
"God **just** do."
Remember you pray to God
JUST and **TRUE**

Poverty

Some people can and some people can't
Some people shall and some people shan't
As for me, it's time to rant
It may even transform into a tantrum
We're all born into the world spectrum
The big difference between the cans and can nots
The shalls and the shall nots
is just how much they've got
At one end of the spectrum
the few people have lots
At the other end there are so many
they collect pennies in pots
Some don't even have a pot to pee in
Let's not forget, we're all human beings
Worldwide poverty is increasing
As the rich get richer and the poor get poorer
A bowl of rice gets smaller and smaller
Ten percent of the world population
Face relentless daily starvation
Living in desperation

100 million people have nowhere to live
They survive on what charity gives
Every day they struggle to manage
Whilst greedy deceits and cheats take advantage
They play the poverty card
They say that life is hard
They say they're looking after orphans
They say we all have more than
But mostly it's a scam
They even threaten to take their own lives
Emotional blackmail with suicide
It leaves me with confusion
Is it real or an illusion?
Whilst the rich indulge in massive feasts
Poverty in the UK is on the increase
More homeless people on the streets
22% live in poverty
Not living properly
Statistics and probability
Drive you to lose your sanity
Their vanity left when their hearts sank
The day they went to the local Foodbank

Poverty does not discriminate with age
Young and old trapped in the cage
4.3 million children is an outrage
Is this really fair?
The world has 2,153 billionaires
They have more than 60% of the world combined
Is that really fine?
The 22 richest men's total capital
Is more than all the women in Africa
If the top 1% of the rich
paid extra tax by half a percent more
That could make all the difference to the poor
After 10 years tax on those billionaires
117 million jobs could provide much needed care
I know this rant is long
I know these words are strong
But come on
Don't you think it's wrong?

"Overcoming poverty is not a gesture of charity. It is an act of justice. It is the protection of a fundamental human right, the right to dignity and a decent life. While poverty persists, there is no true freedom." – Nelson Mandela

Image: John Hain

Drifters

Dedicated to the many Christians that struggle to find a church, commit and put down roots.

A tumbleweed drifts across the plain
The swirling dust just does the same
Endless motion with nothing gained
Senseless emotion can't be contained
Keep on tumbling can't be chained
Or restrained
keep moving hide my stains

You are resistant
want to be different
Keep moving remain ignorant
Pretend you're not belligerent
You're a tumbleweed itinerant
Fearful child, like an infant
You're not a commitment participant

There must come a time
when you stop tumbling

Find where you belong and stop grumbling
You stumble along and keep mumbling
Will you moot
Dispute
then shoot?
It's time to put down roots
If you want to produce fruit

What are you looking for?
What have you found?
Will you find a church that is sound?
Put down your roots on solid ground
Are you in or are you out?
What are you about?
Stop tumbling and shout

Idiosyncrasy

To Keith

Are we free to be who we want to be?
With quirky traits and idiosyncrasy?
Can you appreciate good poetry?
A great poem my friend wrote
It started with this quote
The boy stood on the burning deck
What the heck?
It was his first attempt at rhyme
Composed with a glass of quality wine
[American accent alert]
He sure did it real fine
I'll tell you some more of this friend of mine
He's a really great bloke
that likes a joke
He likes a good laugh
that will be his epitaph
Must be full-caff not decaff
I'm talking coffee
nothing wishy-washy or frothy
If you wonder who this person is
just listen to the clues
"Could do."
"Cuz I want to."
A couple of things my friend does say

Back in the day
He lived in Springfield, USA
His first car a '58 Chevrolet
He drove his Chevy to the levy, it was blue
He drove it, **"Cuz he wanted to."**
Without being rude
he is quite shrewd
He's never lewd
"We don't need that."
It's another phrase from his chat
He's no wombat in an Aussie hat
Do you think you know who my friend is?
This poem is a bit of a quiz
Shall I tell you?
Could do
Here's another clue
He's a rare breed indeed there are few
Fewer and fewer
He engineered the sewers
moving number twoers
My friend is often seen
watching Forest Green – that's Rovers
At his allotment scene
he plants broad beans and digs over clover
If you look underneath a leaf
You might just find my friend called Keith
This poem mentions a few Keith facts
Keith might say, **"We don't need that."**

Last

Inspired by Matthew 20:1-16

I'll tell you a story the rhyming way
This is what the man did say
Please come and work for me today
You will receive a fair day's pay
We agreed a set sum of money
I tell you
this story isn't funny
Stitched up I was, because
I was a berk
There was a lot of work
I kid you not, it's not a joke
The Boss went out to find more folk

Please come and work for me today
You will receive a fair day's pay
In the middle of the day they all arrived
We work hard side by side
There really was plenty of work
But I felt like a complete jerk
Then things got worse
When the job was nearly done
The Boss went out and invited everyone

Please come and work for me today
You will receive a fair day's pay
For just an hour they worked that day
You won't believe what I'm about to say
Now, I don't like to complain
But let me explain
And share my pain
We all got paid the same
Do you think that is fair?
All day long I was there
Then the Boss said
"You've all received as agreed
There's no need to be grieved
Don't be envious if I'm generous
If you don't like it, you'd better leave fast
The last shall be first and the first shall be last."

If you have enjoyed reading this book, please visit
Amazon and/or Goodreads
and leave a quick review.
Thank you.

Please also continue reading for the story of how
God made me a poet and an author.

I Am An Author

This book and the other books that have since followed almost didn't happen. I feel that it is important to include this story in each of my published books, which you will find listed at the back of this book.

My mum died in 2011 and while sorting through her belongings, we found the start of her life story, in her scribbly handwriting. It was only a few pages long, but it expressed her pain and struggles in life. It was inspirational and it planted a small seed in me. I had the idea of doing the same. That idea rolled around in my head for a couple of years, but I questioned it,

"How would I find the time to write"? Life was already busy running a charity (see my book, 'The Golden Thread').

Then, in 2013 I shared my thought with a person that I considered to be a friend. I hoped to receive some encouragement and reassurance that I could do this, but I didn't!

This is how the conversation went:
"I'm thinking of becoming an author."
The response somewhat surprised me, "You couldn't possibly be an author."
I respected this person's opinion so I asked, "Oh, why not?"
"Because authors write 3,600 words in an hour and you could never do that."

It was said with such authority, such confidence and knowledge that I just accepted it. "Your right, I could never do that." I knew that my crippled finger would always slow me down, but I now know that no disability should EVER stop anyone from following a dream. This one throwaway comment would delay my writing like a curse. God was speaking to me, leading me, but a massive barrier had just been built and it would hold me back for years.

In 2015 I stepped down from full-time charity work and managed to free up some time. It was then that I pushed the barrier out of the way and I wrote and published my first book, my biographical story called, 'The Golden Thread'. It felt good to have a book published. I knew that my story could impact the lives of many (and it has) and to share it was a way of glorifying God, but I still struggled to consider myself as an author, with my 'friend's' comment still echoing in my mind, *"You could never be an author."*

In agreement, I now found myself thinking, "Yeah, it's a one-off, a fluke, anyone can write ONE book. It doesn't make you an author."

That then was that, decision made, I'm not an author and it's time to move on. Yet, God is patient and He had other plans, but it would take another three years before I knew exactly what He would require of me.

In 2018 my kidneys had failed so badly that I had been on dialysis for two years. We went to a Christian summer camp festival, called, "Naturally Supernatural". It was organized by

Soul Survivor and this was our third year of attending. Halfway through the week, during the loud worship time, in the throng of thousands of people, I became angry with God. I sat and I cried out aloud, "O God! What am I supposed to be doing with my life? Have you given up on me? Do you no longer have any use for me? Why have you abandoned me?"

Then, amid the noise and hubbub, I heard Him. It wasn't an audible voice; it was like a brain download. Some may say that it was a thought, but it was more, it originated from a supernatural source. It was so powerful, "You still have skills and tools that I have given you! I want you to use them. I haven't finished with you yet."

I felt the warming presence of the Holy Spirit course through me and I instantly knew that God had heard my cry and He had responded, but I still didn't know what it meant. Skills and tools? Did He want me to continue in youth work? He had equipped me for that role, but now it didn't seem right.

Later that week, a woman that I had never met before prayed for me. She told me that she feels that God hasn't finished with me yet. She had a picture of me walking and said, "I believe God wants you to walk with your Gospel shoes on and that you will be ready to speak the good news of the Gospel."

For a brief period, once again I found myself angry and confused. I tried to explain to her, "I have end-stage kidney failure and I'm waiting for a transplant! I don't think I'll be walking far too soon."

I was bang-out-of-order, yet she humbly apologised, "I'm sorry, I'm new to this and maybe I have it wrong."

We both returned to our seats, but something caused me to watch where she went. She was four rows immediately behind where I sat. Now her words echoed around my head, just like the words from five years earlier had echoed, *"You can never be an author."*

She had said, *"God hasn't finished with you yet."* God had told me the same, *"I haven't finished with you yet."* Little did I know, that this was the five-year-old curse being undone, I was being released! *"I have given you tools and skills…"*

My mind raced through my life, "What tools? What skills?" My racing mind stopped in my first year of knowing Jesus and instantly I knew what He was telling me. I ran back four rows to the woman that had prayed for me. "I'm sorry, I need to apologise. God spoke to me through you and I was too angry to hear or understand, but what you said was spot on. I now know that He wants me to write."

In that first year of knowing Jesus, He had given me the gift (tool) and the ability (skill) of rhyming words and I had used it to become a rap artist. That skill had since developed and my writing skills helped me to develop The Door Youth Project charity.

I felt the power of the Holy Spirit already form words in my head; I was so excited! When I went home from Naturally Supernatural, I had the idea to write some teen fiction. I had previously gathered a collection of teen fiction books, which I now intended to read, to gain inspiration. Now, as I pawed my way through the books, I came to an abrupt halt, as I once again heard God's voice in my heart, *"I have given you the tools and skills, now use them!"*

I left the books on the shelf, then doubt tried to have a final word. *"You can NEVER be an author! An author writes 3,600 words an hour!"* Was that true? I decided to Google it and discovered that most authors write 1,000 words in a day. The figure of 3,600 is how many words a copy typist can produce in an hour. I had been cursed and lied to. Now though, I knew the truth and I started to write my first novel. "Issues" was written in just over a month. Then, as soon as it was published, I felt inspired to write, "My Foundation for Life." I had used the skills and the tools but still struggled to call myself an author (the curse was strong) – *"You can never be an author!"* The fire faded in my heart and I didn't write anything for nearly two years (recovering from a kidney transplant slowed me down). Then at the end of my transplant year of 2019, it started to snow and I was once again inspired to write my first science fiction novel. When "The Invasion of the MIMICS" was eventually published, I could at last call myself an 'author'. The curse had been lifted and with it came a full-on release.

Just a month later, I published my poetry book, "Rhyme Time." Soon afterwards, I was in a prayer meeting, when these words came into my head, "ONE GOD – Many names." I instantly had the thought that I had to produce a film (yes, I also make films) with this title. As the film was being made, I also knew that God wanted me to publish a book with the title and so in November 2020, I started to meditate on the many names and titles of God (over 900 in the book). I wrote my thoughts and life-related stories for many of the names and sensed the Holy Spirit's presence grow in me. Then, after just three months and halfway through writing the book, He gave me another 'commission'.

'Commission' is the word that I like to use and I see it as **COM**e together on **MISSION** with God. This time, the call was to use the 'base' writing skill that He had given me *(use the skills and tools)* – 'rhyme'. A friend of mine had recently rewritten Psalm 23 as a rhyming poem. I had produced a poetry book and several 'spoken word' films. Now, I felt God speak to me again, "I gave you these tools and these skills in preparation for this time. Work with me and write the 'Psalms in Rhyme.'"

I write to bless others and to give God the glory and so I was obedient and did as He had commanded. The whole experience was an incredible journey of five months, during which I was immersed in God's presence.

The writing now flowed, like a supernatural river of words. The curse was broken, "I AM AN AUTHOR."

Writing two books at the same time is quite incredible and only possible (for me) with God in the mix, but as if that wasn't enough, He also gave me my first illustrated children's book to produce, "The Land of Make Believe." He continued to pour other poems into my mind regularly, plus He gave me the first four chapters of the sequel to, "The Invasion of the MIMICS."

Just a few negative words telling me that *'I CAN'T'* had held me back, but I had learnt. Never let ANYONE tell you that you can't do something or be something.

**Brendan Conboy has an active speaking
MINISTRY for GOD
And is looking forward to
hearing from you**

*Contact Brendan at the following:
Email – bmconboy@gmail.com
Phone - +44 (0)1453 731008
Mobile – 07980 404873
www.brendanconboy.co.uk*

**The following pages contain information
about Brendan's book titles (Bibliography).**

The Golden Thread – Biography
A true story of fear, forgiveness and faith
First published – 1st September 2015

Brendan Conboy grew up in fear and confusion, struggling with many personal issues. These experiences formed a foundation that could have ended in disaster, but instead, became the motivator to want to make a positive difference.

Issues – Teen / YA Fiction
We all have issues… Can a bully change?
First published – 23rd January 2019

Marcus Daniel was a caring, intelligent, larger-than-average ten-year-old. His parents changed and then so did he. Now Marcus is thirteen years old and a spiteful bully, full of anger, rage and pain. His actions have changed others. Will the fear, pain and rage win?

My Foundation for Life – Semi Biog / Scriptural Teaching
14 underpinning and impacting scriptures
First published – 19th February 2019

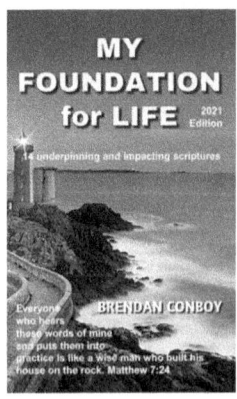

What is it that makes some of us more resilient than others? I am sure that psychologists will have several long-winded explanations to answer this question, but I believe that we can increase our resilience by building our lives on a foundation of truth

Rhyme Time – Poetry
Poems with a message for you to read.
Poems of truth that plant a seed.
First published – 13th November 2020

The Invasion of the MIMICS
Science Fiction / Dystopian / Fantasy
They're already here… Invading your country…
Dwelling in your home… Living in your body!
First published – 21ˢᵗ October 2020

Climate change had been predicted long ago, but not one person could foresee the events that had unfolded. Humanity is defeated, civilization lost, all hope has gone. Enlightenment is the new belief, but there are those who refuse to believe.

The Land of Make Believe – Children's fantasy in rhyme
Based on the story of doubting Thomas
First published – 4ᵗʰ March 2021

ONE GOD Many Names
First published – 14ᵗʰ July 2021

When we meditate on the many names of God, something powerful can happen to us. Brendan Conboy shares his thoughts and personal stories of what some of these names mean and how they had a transformational impact on his life.

The Book of PSALMS in Rhyme
First published – 24ᵗʰ August 2021

**POWERFUL…
POETIC…
RHYTHMIC,
RHYMING
PSALMS…
A fresh expression
to ignite your soul.**

Legacy of the Mimics
First published – 20th June 2022

Book 2 in the Mimics series. Her eyes told her everything was calm, as it should be. Her eyes deceived her. Her mind sensed something else.

Beyond the void

www.ingramcontent.com/pod-product-compliance
Lightning Source LLC
Chambersburg PA
CBHW072056110526
44590CB00018B/3192